Experiments
with a
Ruler

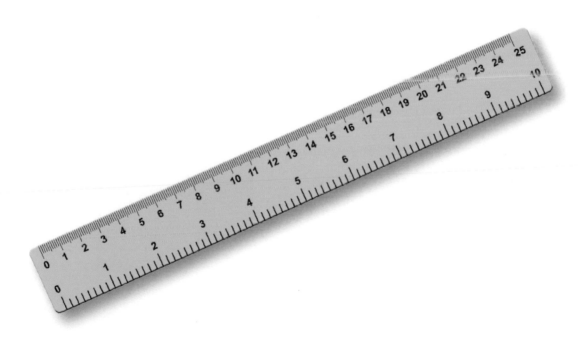

By Angela Royston

A⁺
Smart Apple Media

Published by Smart Apple Media,
an imprint of Black Rabbit Books
P.O. Box 3263, Mankato, Minnesota 56002
www.smartapplemedia.com

Published by arrangement with the
Watts Publishing Group LTD, London.

Cataloging-in-Publication Data is available from the
Library of Congress
ISBN: 978-1-62588-143-4 (library binding)
ISBN: 978-1-68071-016-8 (eBook)

Series editor: Sarah Peutrill
Art director: Jonathan Hair
Design: Matt Lilly and Ruth Walton
Science consultant: Meredith Blakeney
Models: Yusuf Hofri, Samuel Knudsen and
Lyia Sheikh

Credits: 3drenderings/Shutterstock: 17br. Lesha
Bu/Shutterstock: 6b. Paul Fleet/Shutterstock: 21br.
Konstantin Gushcha/Shutterstock: 7t.
Kamira/Shutterstock: 6c. Kzenon/Shutterstock:
16br. Eric Le Francais/Shutterstock: 6r. Matt Lilly:
25b. Mates/Shutterstock: 19br. Phoenix1983/
Shutterstock: 1. Stephen Aaron Rees/
Shutterstock: 6cr. spe/Shutterstock: 27b.
Igor Terekhov/Shutterstock: 6cl. Every attempt has
been made to clear copyright. Should there be
any inadvertent omission please apply to the
publisher for rectification.

Published by arrangement with Franklin Watts,
London.

Printed in the United States of America by CG Book
Printers, North Mankato, Minnesota.

PO1777
3-2016

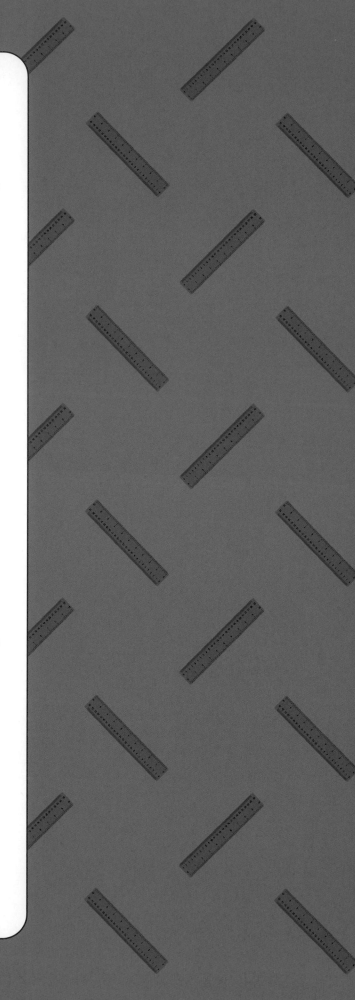

Contents

Words in **bold** are in the glossary on pages 28–29.

What is a Ruler?

A ruler has two long straight edges that are used for drawing straight lines and for measuring length. The long edges of a ruler are marked with a scale that shows inches, centimeters, or other units of measurement.

Kinds of ruler

Many different people, including school children, use a ruler. A school ruler is marked in inches and millimeters. It can measure lengths of up to 12 inches or 30 centimeters. They are easy to use and cheap to buy. A measuring tape is a kind of long ruler that rolls up into a small space. Dressmakers and builders use measuring tapes.

▶ Rulers and measuring tapes are used for measuring how long something is.

▶ This architect's drawing shows how a new house will look.

Architects

Architects are people who design buildings, often on computers. They use rulers to draw **draft** plans of the layout of the building. The plan is a kind of map of each room. It also shows how the building will look from outside.

Builders

Builders use rulers to help them construct or alter a building. They measure doors, walls, floorboards, and other parts of the building. Carpenters are people who make things with wood. They draw straight lines and measure the lengths of pieces of wood before they cut them.

▼ A carpenter carefully measures a length of wood, and marks it with a pencil.

Comparing rulers

Collect rulers of different lengths and made of different materials. How long is the longest ruler? Which one is the bendiest? Which is the most **rigid**? Are any of them **transparent**? What is the advantage of a ruler that is transparent?

◄ Most rulers will bend a bit, but be careful not to bend them too much, or they might break!

The experiments in this book use a ruler to explore forces, **levers, friction,** and other aspects of science—even **air pressure!**

Measuring

People have been measuring things for thousands of years. At first they measured things using parts of their body. They measured short distances using the length of their fingers, hands, or feet. For longer things, they used the length of their stride—a big step—or the width of their outstretched arms.

You will need:
A ruler
A measuring tape

1

Measure your **hand span**. Place the tip of your little finger on "0" on the ruler. Stretch your fingers. How far along the ruler can you reach with your thumb?

Compare the length of your hand span with those of other people. Are they the same?

2

Measure your foot by standing on the ruler with your heel on "0".

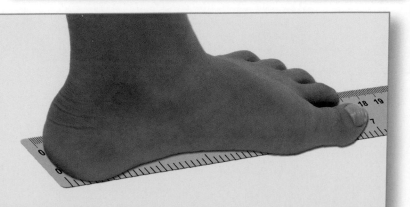

3 Now cross a room by stepping heel to toe. Multiply your foot length by the number of steps it takes. Measure the room with a tape measure. How accurate were you?

4 How long is your stride? Put your heel against a wall and take a big step. Place the ruler where your toes reach. Using the tape measure, find the distance you have stepped from the wall. Now use your stride to measure the width of the room.

Standard measurements

People soon found that using strides and the length of their feet was not accurate enough. Some people had bigger feet than other people! They agreed on **standard** measurements, which they used instead.

Flicking Power

Test several rulers to find out which one can flick a paper ball the farthest. To make the test **fair**, choose or make a mark to stand on when you flick the balls.

You will need:
As many different rulers as you can find
Several sheets of printer paper

1 Fold the paper in half and then in half again lengthwise.

Hold the ruler firmly along each fold and tear the paper into four strips.

2

Fold each strip in half and then in half again. Use the ruler to tear along the folds to make four pieces. Scrunch up each piece of paper to make a ball. Scrunch them to the same size.

3 Examine all the rulers. Which one do you think will flick the balls the farthest? Why?

4 Hold a ball on one end of a ruler. Bend the ruler back as far as it will go easily. Let go of the ball. Now test the other rulers. Record your results. Which one flicked the balls farthest?

 # What happened?

You used **energy** to bend the ruler back. The bent ruler stored the energy until you let it go. Then the energy moved into the ball. The more energy you put into the ruler the farther the ball will fly. The ruler that is both stronger and bendier than the other rulers should flick the balls farthest.

Paper Trick: Air Pressure

It's easy to
lift a sheet of newspaper
with a ruler, or is it?

You will need:
A ruler
A sheet of
    newspaper
A table

1 Place the ruler half on and half off the table.

2 Place the open sheet of newspaper over the ruler. Slowly push down the free end of the ruler. Is it easy to lift the paper?

3 Repeat the experiment, but this time give the free end a sharp tap. What happens?

What happened?

Air presses down on the whole surface of the paper. This is called air pressure. When you push the ruler down slowly, the air moves out of the way. When you hit it quickly, the air doesn't have time to move away, so air pressure holds the paper down.

Who is Faster?

This experiment tests how quickly you react; that is how quickly your brain and body work together.

1 One person holds the ruler vertically with the 12 inch (30 cm) mark at the top. The other person holds their hand ready at the bottom but not touching the ruler, as shown in the photo.

2 Without warning, the first person lets go of the ruler and the second person catches it. Look at where their thumb is on the ruler and make a note of the nearest inch or centimeter.

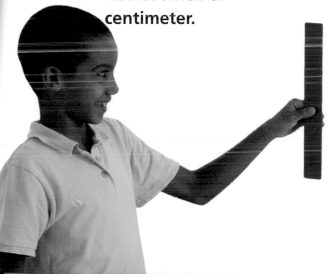

3 Try again. Is the catcher quicker this time? The smaller the number, the faster the time.

4 Swap roles. Who is faster?

Brain power

The more often you do something, the faster you get. Your brain learns what to do and gets quicker at telling your fingers to move.

A Lifting Machine

A lever is a simple machine that allows you to lift a heavy **load** more easily. This experiment uses a ruler as a lever. If possible, do this experiment outside!

You will need:
A strong 12-inch (30 cm) ruler
A can of beans
A small bucket or container with a handle
A pitcher of water
A measuring cup
A table

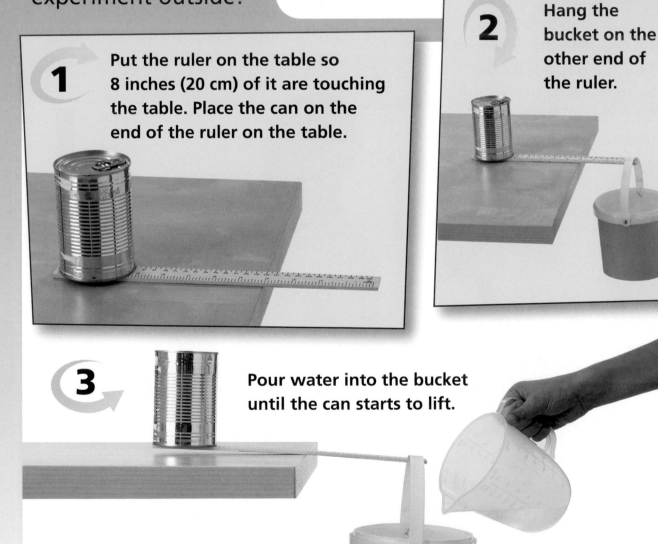

1 Put the ruler on the table so 8 inches (20 cm) of it are touching the table. Place the can on the end of the ruler on the table.

2 Hang the bucket on the other end of the ruler.

3 Pour water into the bucket until the can starts to lift.

4 Pour the water from the bucket into the measuring cup and note how much there is. Empty the water back into the pitcher.

5 Move the ruler so 6 inches (15 cm) are touching the table. Repeat the experiment.

Now move the ruler until only 4 inches (10 cm) are touching the table and repeat the experiment. What do you notice about the amount of water you need to lift the can each time?

6 Make a graph to show your results.

What happened?

The less water you need to add to the bucket, the smaller the force needed to lift the can. You should have found that the least force was needed when the "handle" of the lever (the part hanging over the table) was longest.

Turning point

A lever allows you to lift a load by pushing down. In this experiment the ruler is a lever. It turns around the **fulcrum**—in this case the edge of the table.

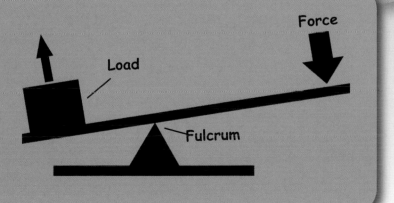

Force

Load

Fulcrum

Comparing Levers

Experiment with levers and see what you can find out. Here are some suggestions to start with.

You will need:
Selection of different rulers, including a 12-inch (30 cm) ruler
A load, for example, a heavy book

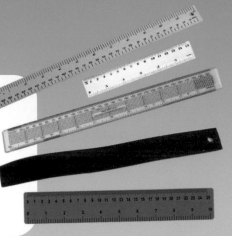

1 Experiment with rulers of different lengths. Which makes the best lever?

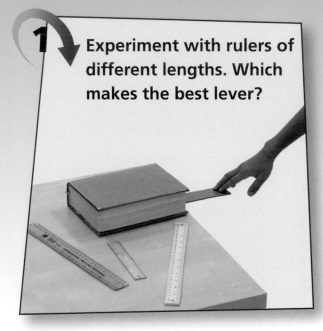

Everyday levers

Many everyday tools are levers. For example, a shovel is a lever. A pair of scissors is two levers working together.

2 Which is better: a rigid (stiff) ruler or a bendy ruler?

3 Is it easier to lift the load when it is close to the fulcrum or when it is far from the fulcrum?

▲ This man is pushing the handle of the shovel down to lift up the load of soil.

Make a Catapult

In ancient times, armies used **catapults**, a kind of lever, to attack castles and the people inside them. You can make a simple catapult using a ruler and an eraser.

You will need:
A ruler
An eraser
Paper balls (see page 10)

1 Place the ruler over the eraser so that the eraser is at the 3-inch (8 cm) mark.

2 Place a ball at the 12-inch (30 cm) mark.

3 Flick the short end down. What happens? Did it go mostly forward or upward?

▲ The end of this catapult is bent down by winding the rope. Then the rope is let go.

Seesaws

Use a ruler and an eraser to make a seesaw and compare the weights of different things.

1 Balance the ruler on the eraser, so it is level and steady.

2

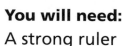

Put an object at each end of the ruler. Does the ruler stay balanced, or does one end go down and the other up?

3 Which of the objects do you think will be the heaviest and which the lightest? Test them on the ruler. Were you right?

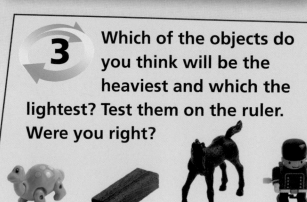

What happened?

The ruler tilted down on the side of the heavier object. The ruler stayed balanced when the objects on each end were the same weight. The lightest object will never tilt down.

Money Scales

1 Balance the ruler on the eraser, so it is level and steady.

3 How many 5¢ coins does it take to balance a 25¢ coin? Try other combinations.

2 Place a coin of the same value on each end. Does the ruler balance?

Vending machines
Vending machines can tell the value of any coin dropped into them. They are programmed to recognize various things, including the weight of the coin.

Balancing Unequal Weights

How can you balance two unequal weights? Simply by changing their positions on the ruler!

You will need:
A strong ruler
An eraser
Objects, such as coins, that weigh different amounts

1 Balance the ruler on the eraser, so it is level and steady.

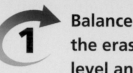

2 Put two objects, one heavier than the other, on each end of the ruler. Now move the heavier object toward the eraser. Find the place on the ruler where it balances the lighter object.

3 Draw a diagram to show the position of the objects on the ruler when they balance.

4 Try again, but this time slide the ruler along the eraser until it is balanced again. Which weight is closer to the fulcrum (the eraser)?

5

Draw a diagram to show the positions of the objects and the ruler on the eraser.

6

Repeat both experiments with different weights.

What happened?

A seesaw is a lever that is balanced on the fulcrum. The farther a weight is from the fulcrum, the larger the force it exerts. Moving the heavier load toward the fulcrum meant that the smaller force produced by the lighter load became strong enough to balance the heavier load. You get the same result when you move the fulcrum closer to the heavier load.

▼ A crane has a heavy counterweight that moves along the jib to balance the weight of the load.

Counterweight

Jib

Load

Ramps

Use a ruler to make a **ramp** for rolling marbles down. Before you start, test different rulers to see which one makes the best ramp.

You will need:
A ruler
A strip of paper as long as the ruler and twice as wide
A tape measure
Books
A marble
Graph paper and pencil

1 Place the ruler along the middle of the strip of paper and bend up each side.

Make a pile of books about 0.5 inch (1 cm) high. Measure the exact height of the pile. Prop the end of the ruler against the books.

2 Note the place on the ruler where it touches the edge of the top book. To make the test fair, you need to place the ruler at this same place each time.

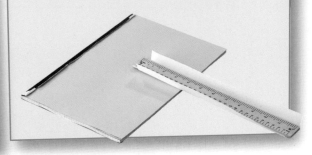

3 Hold the marble at the top of the ruler and let it go.

4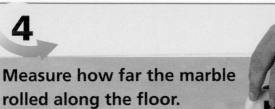

Measure how far the marble rolled along the floor.

5

Now add some more books to the pile. Measure the height of the pile. Do you think the marble will roll farther or less far this time?

6 Measure how far the marble rolls along the floor. Were you right?

7

Keep adding books to the pile and measuring how far the marble rolls. Make a graph to show how far the marble rolled for each height of the ramp.

What happened?

The steeper the ramp, the faster the marble rolls, so the farther it should travel over the table. Try using a smaller or larger marble. Which one goes farther on the same ramp?

Testing Different Surfaces

Change the surface that the marble rolls along after it leaves the ruler ramp (see page 22). Try at least four different surfaces, such as a carpet, piece of cloth, a wooden floor, and a flat path, or playground.

You will need:
A ruler
A measuring tape
A marble
A variety of surfaces
Graph paper and pencil

1 Make a list of the surfaces you have chosen. Put them in order from roughest to smoothest. Which one do you think will allow the marble to roll farthest? Which one the least far?

2 Decide what you have to do to make the test fair.

3 Test each surface and measure how far the marble rolls on each surface.

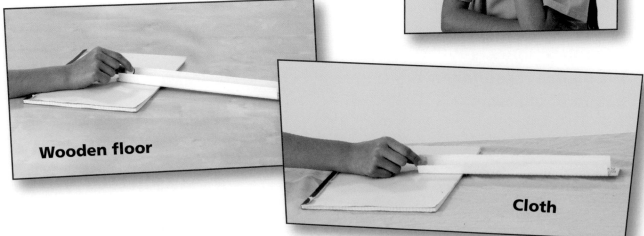

Wooden floor

Cloth

4

Make a bar chart to show how the different surfaces compared.

5

Which allowed the marble to roll farther, the smooth surfaces or the rough surfaces?

What happened?

The marble should have rolled farthest on the smoothest surface. This is because there is less friction between the marble and a smooth surface. Friction slows down and stops one surface moving over another surface.

▼ Ice hockey is a fast game. The ice is so smooth that the **puck** and the players move across it very easily.

Making it Hum

Spin a ruler to make a humming noise. Do this experiment outside, where you will not hit anything or anybody.

You will need:
A ruler
String
A drill or other
sharp object, such as
an awl, corkscrew, or kabob
skewer

1 Ask an adult to drill a hole at each end of the ruler.

2 Cut a piece of string about 15 to 20 inches (40 to 50 cm) long.

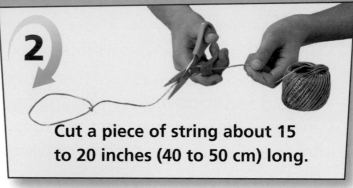

3 Thread the string through one of the holes. Make sure you tie the string securely, so the ruler does not fly off.

4

Hold the string about 4 to 5.5 inches (10 to 14 cm) from the knot and spin the ruler around as fast as you can above your head.

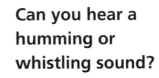

Can you hear a humming or whistling sound?

What happened?

As you spun the ruler, the air passed through the hole faster than the spinning ruler. This made the humming noise.

Try adding more holes to the ruler and spin it again. Has the sound changed?

Humming top

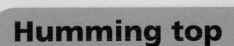

A humming top works in a similar way. This toy has several holes that make the humming sound. The faster the toy spins, the higher the note of the hum.

air pressure force produced by the weight of air pressing on something.

catapults machines that throw stones or other missiles. In the past, large catapults were used to attack castles.

draft a rough plan or first attempt at writing or an illustration.

energy the power to make something happen.

fair the same for every individual. A fair test is one in which everything is kept the same, except for the thing being tested.

friction the force produced when one surface rubs against another surface.

fulcrum the point around which a lever turns.

hand span the distance between your outstretched thumb and little finger.

levers simple machines that allow you to use less force to lift a heavy weight.

load something that is lifted or carried.

puck rubber object that is used in ice hockey, like a ball is in soccer.

ramp a slope.

rigid stiff, not bendy.

standard A standard unit of measurement is one that is accepted and used by most people.

transparent see-through.

Further Information

Websites

www.bitesizephysics.com/Experiments/popsicl-a-pult.html
Build a working catapult using Popsicle sticks, tape, and a rubber band.

phet.colorado.edu/sims/projectile-motion/projectile-motion_en.html
Use this game to try and predict the effects of angle, speed, and mass on objects fired from a cannon.

www.stevespanglerscience.com/lab/experiments/balancing-glass-trick
This amazing trick uses common objects to balance a glass of water and seemingly defy the laws of science.

Note to parents and teachers: The publisher has made every effort to ensure that these websites are suitable for children. However, due to the nature of the Internet, we strongly advise the supervision of web access by a responsible adult.

Books

Forces and Motion in the Real World by Kathleen M. Muldoon, Abdo Publishing Company, 2013

The Gripping Truth About Forces and Motion by Agnieszka Biskup and Bernice Lum, Fact Finders, 2012

Thud!: Wile E. Coyote Experiments with Forces and Motion by Mark Weakland and Christian Cornia, Warner Bros., 2014

Index